# The Power of Now Journal

# 當下力量的
# 靜心導引

## 斬斷苦惱，找回每時每刻的自己！

艾克哈特·托勒（Eckhart Tolle） 著

# 目錄
# contents

When you are on a journey, it is certainly helpful to know
where you are going...but don't forget: the only thing that
is ultimately real about your journey is

*the step that you are taking at this moment.*

在人生旅程上，知道自己要去哪裡或至少知道大方向，
當然是很重要的。但別忘了，這趟旅程唯一一件最真實的事，
就是這一刻你即將踏出的這一步。

你的內在旅程只需要一步——
你此時此刻踏出的這一步。

*Your inner journey only has one step:*
the step you are taking right now.

保持臨在，

繼續觀察，

守護好自己的內在空間。

*Stay present, stay conscious.*
Be the ever-alert guardian
of your inner space.

好消息是，你可以從心智的束縛中解脫，

這是唯一的真正解脫。

而你現在就可以做到。

*The good news is* that you *can* free yourself from your mind.
This is the only true liberation.
You can take the first step right now.

唯有當下可以等你擺脫過去的桎梏。

更多的時間無法讓你擺脫時間。

*Only the present can free you* of the past.

More time cannot free you of time.

取用當下的力量才是關鍵所在。

Access the power of Now. That is the key.

不採取行動 是因為恐懼嗎？

如果是，那就承認、觀察、專注於那份恐懼，

*Is fear preventing you* from taking action?

Acknowledge the fear, watch it,

全然臨在時也帶著它，

　　這將會斬斷恐懼與你的思維之間的連結。

take your attention into it, be fully present with it.

　　Doing so cuts the link between the fear and your thinking.

我談到了人類意識的深刻變化，
那並非一個遙不可及的夢想，
無論你是誰或身處何處，當下就可以達成。

I speak of a profound transformation of human
consciousness — not as a distant future possibility,
but available now — no matter who or where you are.

在你未能持續地保持臨在、全然處於意識清明狀態之前，
你將會在有意識狀態與無意識狀態、
臨在狀態與認同心智狀態之間，來回擺盪一陣子。

*You shift back and forth for a while* between consciousness
and unconsciousness, between the state of presence
and the state of mind identification.

你失落了當下，又重拾它，周而復始，
　　直到最後臨在成了主導狀態。

You lose the Now, and you return to it, again and again.
Eventually, presence becomes your predominant state.

觀照呼吸的韻律，感受氣息的進出，
　　感受身體裡面的能量，
　　讓一切如其所是，無論內外。

*Observe the rhythm of your breathing;* feel the air
　　flowing in and out, feel the life energy inside your body.
　　Allow everything to be, within and without.

容許所有事物以其本然樣貌呈現，深深地進入當下。

Allow the "isness" of all things. *Move deeply into the Now.*

覺知到使各種事物存在的空間本身。

聆聽每一種聲音，但不要加以評斷。

*Be aware of the space* that allows everything to be.

Listen to the sounds; don't judge them.

聆聽各種聲音底下的寂靜。觸摸一些東西，
什麼都可以，去感受並承認它的存在狀態。

Listen to the silence underneath the sounds. Touch
something — anything — and feel and acknowledge its Being.

就在你開始觀看這個思考者的那一刻，
一種更高層次的意識就會啟動。
你將會明白，有一種超越思維之上的智性存在……

The moment you start *watching the thinker*, a higher level of
consciousness becomes activated. You then begin to
realize that there is a vast realm of intelligence beyond thought....

你將會發現，對你來說，真正重要的東西——
美、愛、創造力、喜悅、內在平安——
都是從比思維更高的層次應運而生。

你就開始覺醒了。

You also realize that all the things that truly matter — beauty, love,
creativity, joy, inner peace — arise from beyond the mind.

*You begin to awaken.*

專注是轉化的關鍵，全然地專注意味著接納。

專注就像一束光，意識的專注力量可以

將任何東西轉化為意識。

Attention is the key to transformation — and full attention
also implies acceptance. Attention is like a beam of light —
the focused power of your consciousness that

*transmutes everything into itself.*

只要不去抗拒生命，就能活在輕鬆自在的恩典狀態裡。
在這種狀態下，你不再依賴外物必須以特定方式呈現，
才能稱得上好或壞。

To offer no resistance to life is to be in a state of grace, ease,
and lightness. This state is then no longer dependent
upon things being in a certain way, good or bad.

我所訴說的靈性真理，
　　無一不是你內心深處早已了知的。
　我所能夠做的，僅僅是提醒你早已遺忘的事情。

I cannot tell you any spiritual truth
that deep within you don't know already.
All I can do is remind you of what you have forgotten.

你將學到如何從心智的框框中解脫，
進入開悟的意識狀態，
並在日常生活中保持不墜。

*You are shown how to free yourself* from enslavement
to the mind, enter into this enlightened
state of consciousness and sustain it in everyday life.

開悟總是被想成一種艱難的超凡成就，
而小我總喜歡唆使人這樣看待開悟。
事實上，開悟只是一種自然而至的狀態，
一種讓人感受到與本體合一的狀態。

*The word "enlightenment"* conjures up the idea of some super-human accomplishment, and the ego likes to keep it that way, but it is simply your natural state of *felt* oneness with Being.

當下乃是一把開啟解脫的鑰匙。

不過只要你繼續認同於心智，你就無法尋得當下此刻。

*The present moment holds the key* to liberation. But you cannot find the present moment as long as you *are* your mind.

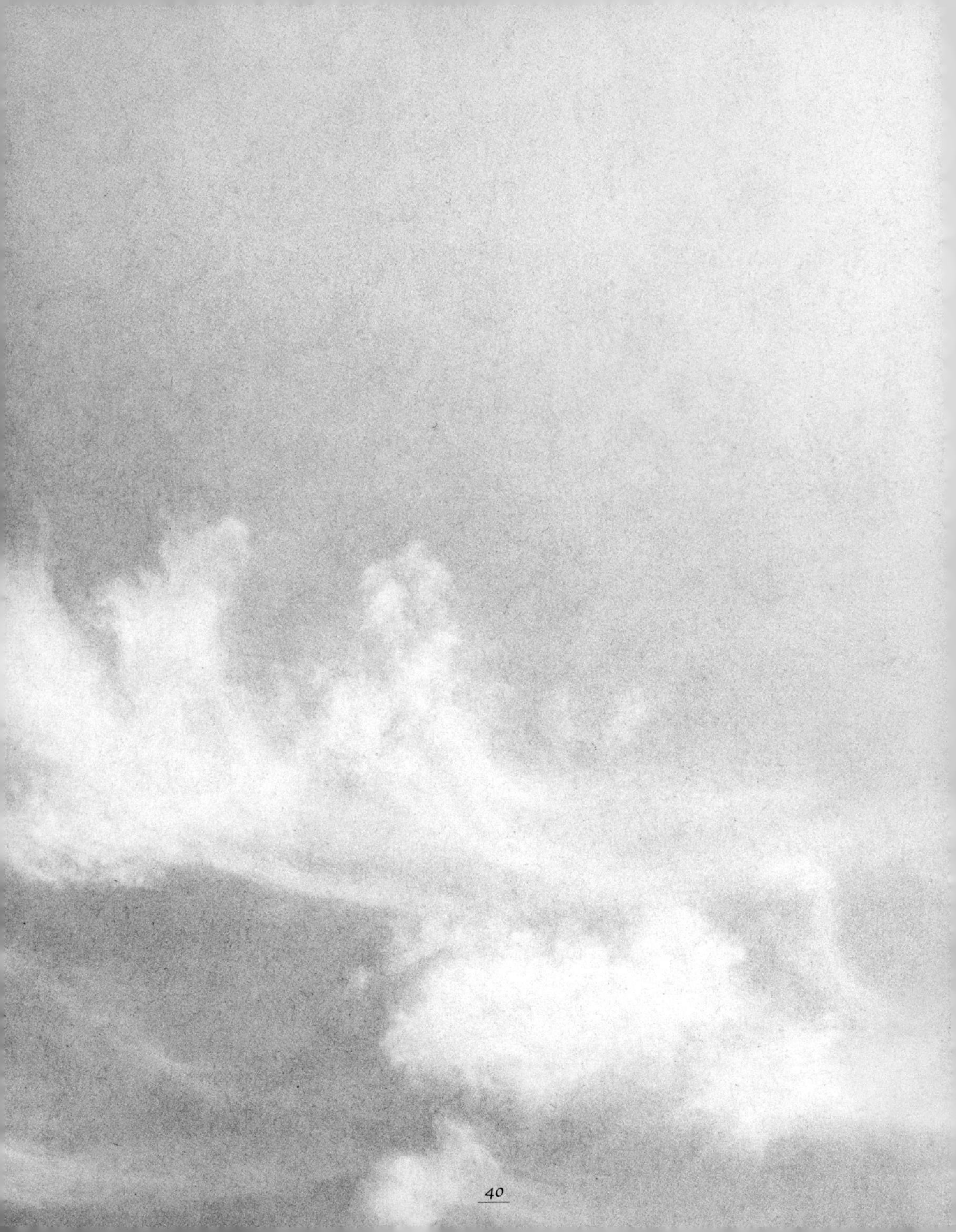

所謂寬恕，就是認清了過去的虛妄不實，
並允許當下此刻如其所是。
透過寬恕，轉化的奇蹟將不只發生於外在，
也會發生於內在。

*Through forgiveness,* which essentially means recognizing
the insubstantiality of the past and allowing
the present moment to be as it is, the miracle of
transformation happens not only within but also without.

如果你突然感覺到很輕鬆、很清明，
內心充滿平安，就代表你已真正臣服了。

If you suddenly feel very light, clear, and deeply at peace, that is

an unmistakable *sign that you have truly surrendered.*

每當你在思緒之流中成功創造出一次間隙，

你的意識散發出的光芒就更耀眼。

Every time you create a gap in the stream of mind,
the light of *your consciousness grows stronger.*

# 你正在汙染世界，還是清理世界？

只有你能夠對自己的內在空間負責，
其他人無法代替你，就像你必須對這個地球負責一樣。

如果人能夠清理自己的內在染汙，
自然就會停止製造一切外在汙染了。

*Are you polluting the world or cleaning up the mess?*

You are responsible for your inner space; nobody else is,
just as you are responsible for the planet.

As within, so without: If humans clear inner pollution,
then they will also cease to create outer pollution.

不臣服的態度會僵化你的心理形相，
那是小我的堅硬外殼，
製造出強烈的人我分離感。

*Non-surrender hardens your psychological form,*
the shell of the ego, and so creates
a strong sense of separateness.

開悟意味著超越思維之上，
不掉入比思維更低的層次。

Enlightenment means rising above thought,
not falling back to a level below thought.

Instead of "watching the thinker," you can also create
a gap in the mind stream simply by directing the
focus of your attention into the Now. Just become

*intensely conscious of the present moment.*

若想在思緒之流中創造關係，
除了「觀看這個思考者」之外，還有另一個方法——
專注於當下，也就是令神貫注在此時此刻。

當你進入臨在之中，
任何情緒都會迅速消退並獲得轉化。

Any emotion that you take your presence into
will quickly *subside and become transmuted.*

如果你發覺自己很難直接進入當下，
那就從觀察心智「想從當下逃離」的傾向開始。
你會發現自己總是把未來想得比現在更好或更壞。

*If you find it hard to enter the Now directly,*
start by observing the habitual tendency of your mind
to want to escape from the Now.
You will observe that the future is usually imagined
as either better or worse than the present.

事實是，唯一有力量的時刻只有當下。

The truth is that the only power there is,
is contained within this moment:
*It is the power of your presence.*

問問自己，這一刻有任何讓你苦惱的「問題」嗎？

不是明年，不是明天，也不是五分鐘之後。

而是當下這一刻有什麼不對勁嗎？

*Ask yourself what "problem" you have right now*,

not next year, tomorrow, or five minutes from now.

What is wrong with *this moment*?

每當你注意到，你裡面有某種形式的負面或消極之感出現了，
不要因此認為自己又失敗了，而該視之為一個有利的訊號，
提醒著你：「醒過來吧！跳脫你的心智，臨在當下。」

Whenever you notice that some form of negativity has
arisen within you, look on it not as a failure,
but as a helpful signal that is telling you:

"Wake up. Get out of your mind. Be present."

*Observe the many ways in which* unease, discontent, and
tension arise within you through unnecessary judgment,
resistance to what *is*, and denial of the Now.
Anything unconscious dissolves when you shine the light of consciousness on it.

觀察內心升起的不自在、不滿足和緊張感，
觀察你是如何抗拒本然和否定當下。
任何無意識都會在意識之光的照耀下瓦解。

我是被窗外小鳥的啁啾聲叫醒的。
那是一種彷彿我從未聽過的聲音。

I was awakened by the chirping of a bird outside the window.
I had never heard such a sound before.

我的雙眼還緊閉著，卻看見了一顆珍貴鑽石的影像。

是啊，如果鑽石能發出聲音，
那一定就是我聽到的那個聲音了。

My eyes were still closed, and I saw the image of a
precious diamond. Yes, if a diamond could make a sound,
this is what it would be like.

如果你活得夠久，就會知道「不對勁」乃人之常情。
然而，也正是在逆境中，人最需要學會臣服，
如此，才能化解你的痛苦與悲傷。

If you have lived long enough, you will know that things
"go wrong" quite often. It is precisely at those times
that surrender needs to be practiced if you want to
*eliminate pain and sorrow from your life.*

永遠對當下此刻說「是」。

向本然臣服吧，向人生臣服吧。

如此，你將會赫然發現，

生命開始為你工作，不再與你作對了。

*Always say "yes" to the present moment.* Surrender to what *is*. Say "yes" to life — and see how life suddenly starts working for you rather than against you.

這世上沒有任何事物比寂靜更接近神了。
你所需要做的只是 聆聽寂靜。

It has been said that nothing in this world is so like God as silence.

All you have to do is *pay attention to it.*

聆聽寂靜將會在你的內在創造默觀，
而默觀就是臨在，
就是擺脫了思維形相的意識。

What is stillness other than presence,

*consciousness freed from thought forms?*

有很多方法可以在不間斷的思緒之流中 製造間隙，
靜心冥想即為其一。

*There are many ways to create a gap* in the incessant stream of thought. This is what meditation is all about.

無論身處何處，聆聽寂靜乃是進入臨在最簡單、最直接的方法。
即使是滿布噪音之處，
你也能在聲音之間或聲音底下找到寂靜。

Even if there is noise, there is always some silence underneath
and in between the sounds. Listening to the silence
*immediately creates stillness inside you.*

臨在就是純粹意識，
　　是從心智、形相世界中奪回的意識。

*Presence is pure consciousness* — consciousness that has been reclaimed from the mind, from the world of form.

地球上除了人類之外，
沒有其他生命形式知道什麼是負面性，
一如沒有其他生命形式會去荼毒賴以生存的地球。

*No other life-form* on the planet knows negativity,
only humans, just as no other life-form violates
and poisons the Earth that sustains it.

趁日子還算平順的時候，
把更多的意識帶入日常生活中，非常重要。
一旦這樣做，你臨在的能力會愈來愈強。

It is essential to bring more consciousness into your life
in ordinary situations when everything
is going relatively smoothly. In this way,

*you grow in presence power.*

慈悲就是體認到你與一切萬物有著深層的連結。

*Compassion is the awareness* of a deep bond
between yourself and all creatures.

學習當個煉金術師，把金屬轉化成黃金，
把痛苦轉化為清明意識，把苦難轉化為開悟。

*Become an alchemist.* Transmute base metal into gold,
suffering into consciousness, disaster into enlightenment.

去觀察植物和動物，讓牠們教導你如何學習接納本然，
臣服當下。讓牠們教導你何謂本體，何謂身心統一。

*Watch any plant or animal* and let it teach you
acceptance of what is, surrender to the Now.
Let it teach you Being.

每當思緒之流中出現間隙，
我們就有可能瞥見愛、喜悅、
或是一剎那的深度平安。

*Glimpses of love and joy* or brief moments of deep peace
are possible whenever a gap occurs in the stream of thought.

我張開眼睛，第一道晨曦穿過窗簾照射進來。
我沒有思考，但就是知道，
光所涵蓋的層面遠比我們所知的多得多。

The first light of dawn was filtering through the curtains.
Without any thought, I felt, I knew,
that there is infinitely more to light than we realize.

那道透過窗簾照射進來的柔和光線，
就是「愛」本身。

That soft luminosity filtering through the
curtains was love itself.

充分運用你的感官，安住於你所在之處，環顧四周，
但只是觀看，不要加以詮釋。
看看光線、形狀、顏色、質地，
覺知到各種事物的寂靜臨在。

Use your senses fully: Be where you are. Look around — just look,
don't interpret. See the light, shapes, colors, textures.
*Be aware of the silent presence of each thing.*

你應該養成習慣，隨時問自己：
「此刻，我的內在有什麼樣的情緒？」
這個問題將把你帶往正確的方向。

*Make it a habit to ask yourself:*
What's going on inside me at this moment?
That question will point you in the right direction.

問題都是心智虛構出來的，
需要「時間」才能維生，無法存活於當下。
把你的注意力放在當下，
告訴我，這一刻，你有什麼問題呢？

Problems are mind-made and need time to survive.
They cannot survive in the actuality of the Now.
Focus your attention on the Now and tell me
what problem you have at this moment.

你應該試著暫時忘卻你的人生處境，轉而專注在你的生命上。

你的人生處境存在於時間之中；你的生命卻存在於當下。

你的人生處境是心智虛構之物；你的生命卻是真實不虛的。

Forget about your life situation and pay attention to your *life*.
Your life situation exists in time. Your life is now.
Your life situation is mind-stuff. *Your life is real.*

一種靜默卻強烈的臨在，可以瓦解心智的無意識模式。
當這種能量充盈內在，各種無意識模式也許會暫時殘存，
卻再也無法擺布你的生活。

*It is a silent but intense presence* that dissolves
the unconscious patterns of the mind.
They may still remain active for a while,
but they won't run your life anymore.

在你進入臨在之前，你什麼都不需要知道。

There is nothing that you need to understand
before you can become present.

洗手時，專注於感知每一個動作：
雙手來回的搓洗移動、水的聲音、水的觸感、
肥皂的氣味等等。

*When you wash your hands, pay attention*
to all the sense perceptions associated with the activity:
the sound and feel of the water, the movement of your hands,
the scent of the soap, and so on.

沒有事情發生在過去；事情只發生在當下。

沒有事情發生在未來；事情只發生在當下。

Nothing ever happened in the past; it happened in the Now.
Nothing will ever happen in the future;

*it will happen in the Now.*

有意識地選擇開悟，
就是選擇放下對過去和未來的執著，
將生命聚焦於當下。

Enlightenment consciously chosen means to relinquish
your attachment to past and future and to

*make the Now the main focus of your life.*

當你意識到本體，本體同時就意識到它自己；
當本體意識到它自己，就成了臨在。

When you become conscious of Being, what is really
happening is that Being becomes conscious of itself.
When Being becomes conscious of itself — *that's presence.*

喜悅是沒有緣由的，它只能從本體的喜悅裡自然升起。

喜悅是內在平安的主要部分，

那種境界即是所謂「神的平安」。

*Joy is uncaused and arises from within* as the joy of Being.

It is an essential part of the inner state of peace,

the state that has been called the peace of God.

這是你的自然狀態，無需辛苦爭取或努力達到。

It is your natural state, not something that you need
to work hard for or struggle to attain.

覺知身體可以幫助你保持臨在，讓你定錨於當下。

*Body awareness* keeps you present. It anchors you in the Now.

世界是相互連結的。
當人類的集體意識獲得轉化，
自然界和動物王國同樣也會映照出這種轉化。

這指出了另一種完全不同的世界的可能性。

Since all worlds are interconnected,
when collective human consciousness becomes transformed,

nature and the animal kingdom will reflect that transformation.
This points to the possibility of a completely
different order of reality.

要認識到思考者之下有本體，心智噪音之下有默觀，
痛苦之下有愛、喜樂、自由、救贖與開悟。

To know yourself as the Being underneath the thinker,
the stillness underneath the mental noise,
the love and joy underneath the pain,

*is freedom, salvation, enlightenment.*

臨在抑走了時間。

沒有了時間，痛苦或任何負面性都不復存在。

*Presence removes time.*

Without time, no suffering, no negativity, can survive.

只要持之以恆的去實踐，靜默和平安的感受就會愈來愈深。

事實上，它的深度是無止境的。

你將會感受到有一種精微的喜悅從內在深處升起，

那即是「本體的喜悅」。

With practice, the sense of stillness and peace will deepen.

In fact, there is no end to its depth.

You will also feel a subtle emanation of

*joy arising from deep within: the joy of Being.*

這使萬事萬物存在的寂靜空間不只在外，
也在我們之內。當你全然臨在，就會與它相會。
它就是你裡面無念的內在空間。

*That stillness and vastness* that enables
the universe to *be*…is also within you.
When you are utterly and totally present, you encounter
it as the still inner space of no-mind.

除了此時此刻，

你做的任何事都不會讓你得到救贖。

這對心智來說是難以理解的，

它總以為任何有價值的事都存在於未來。

*There is nothing you can ever do or attain*
that will get you closer to salvation than it is at this moment.
This may be hard to grasp for a mind accustomed to
thinking that everything worthwhile is in the future.

當你完全接納事物的本然，

你就終結了人生中的所有戲碼。

When you live in complete acceptance of what *is*,

that is the *end of all drama in your life.*

如果你能把注意力從空間中的事物上收回來，
你放在心智形相上的注意力就會隨之自動轉移。換言之，
你不可能一邊思考，一邊意識到空間或寂靜。

If you withdraw attention from *things* — objects in
space — you automatically withdraw attention from your
mind objects as well. In other words: You cannot think

and *be aware of space — or of silence.*

愛是本體的一種狀態。

你的愛不在外頭，而是深藏於你之內。

你不可能失去愛，愛也不可能離開你。

愛不會依賴某個人，也不會依賴某個形相。

Love is a state of Being. Your love is not outside; it is
deep within you. You can never lose it, and it cannot leave you.
It is not dependent on some other body,
some external form.

你內在的平安是如此深厚，
以致任何不平安的念頭都自動瓦解了，
彷彿它們從未存在過。

*Your peace is so vast and deep* that anything that is not peace disappears into it as if it had never existed.

不論你自己有沒有意識到，
每一個接近你的人都會被你的臨在觸動，
被你散發的內在平安影響。

Everybody you come in contact with will be touched by your

presence and affected by the peace that you emanate,

*whether they are conscious of it or not.*

BC1071R

# 當下力量的靜心導引： 斬斷苦惱，找回每時每刻的自己！
The Power of Now Journal

作者 艾克哈特·托勒（Eckhart Tolle）
責任編輯 田哲榮
協力編輯 劉芸蓁
封面設計 斐類設計
美術設計 黃淑雅

發行人 蘇拾平
總編輯 于芝峰
副總編輯 田哲榮
業務發行 王綬晨、邱紹溢
行銷企劃 陳詩婷
出版 橡實文化 ACORN Publishing
　　地址：10544臺北市松山區復興北路333號11樓之4
　　電話：02-2718-2001 傳真：02-2719-1308
　　網址：www.acornbooks.com.tw
　　E-mail信箱：acorn@andbooks.com.tw
發行 大雁出版基地
　　地址：10544臺北市松山區復興北路333號11樓之4
　　電話：02-2718-2001 傳真：02-2718-1258
　　讀者傳真服務：02-2718-1258
　　讀者服務信箱：andbooks@andbooks.com.tw
　　劃撥帳號：19983379 戶名：大雁文化事業股份有限公司

印刷 中原造像股份有限公司
二版一刷 2023年4月
定價 360元
ISBN 978-626-7085-85-1
版權所有·翻印必究（Printed in Taiwan）
如有缺頁、破損或裝訂錯誤，請寄回本公司更換。

**國家圖書館出版品預行編目（CIP）資料**

當下力量的靜心導引：斬斷苦惱，找回每
時每刻的自己！/艾克哈特 托勒(Eckhart
Tolle)著. -- 二版. -- 臺北市：橡實文化出版
：大雁出版基地發行, 2023.04
　　面； 公分
譯自 : The power of now Journal
ISBN 978-626-7085-85-1(平裝)

1.CST: 靈修

192.1　　　　　　　　　112001808